CLASSIC COACHES
A Colour Portfolio
Kevin Lane
Ian Allan
PUBLISHING
PRIVATE
SCHOOL BUS
PRIVATE
PRIVATE
76_ NMB
PRIVATE
4401 NX
AEP 849
BEP 691

Introduction

In everything except name, this book is a second *Heyday of the Classic Coach*, originally published back in 1994 and recently reprinted. That first volume was arranged by chassis type, from AEC through to Tilling-Stevens, and roughly covered types built in the early postwar period up to the end of the 1960s.

In this volume I have put the emphasis more on the operator than on the vehicle itself, although I hope that I have included enough variety in the latter, given that AEC, Bedford, Ford and Leyland certainly dominated the coaching scene throughout the 1950s and 1960s. I have also stretched the timescale a little compared with the first book, to include a few more vehicles built during the 1970s and running into the 1980s; I think that the most modern example to be featured is a W-registration Bristol LHS which was new in 1981. Many of the so-called 'classic' types had long production runs. The AEC Reliance was built between 1953 and 1979 and the Leyland Leopard first became available in 1959 and continued until 1982. Bedford's successor to the OB was the ubiquitous SB, which lasted some 36 years until the last were built in 1986. I therefore feel that later examples of these models can be regarded as classics of their type, just as worthy of inclusion as ones built earlier.

The postwar coaching scene was certainly one of growth and change. Restrictions on private motoring ensured plenty of work for operators after the war as tours and excursions were planned and express and limited-stop services resumed. Furthermore, road travel was cheaper than the railways, themselves war-ravaged. This expansion was hampered by a chronic lack of new vehicles, as prewar rolling stock was patched up to work another season or two. The situation eased, of course, and, as the 1950s progressed, coaching entered a golden age. New underfloor-engined coaches took to the road, often accompanied by stylish, modern bodywork, presenting a glamorous image of contemporary coaching. The decade also saw the emergence of a public shop window for the industry in the shape of the annual rallies at Brighton and Blackpool.

By the 1960s, we had entered the motorway age, and with it came longer and more powerful coaches. We had the six-wheel Bedford VAL, double-deckers, and, by the end of this decade, the formation of the National Bus Company. Many old, familiar and much-loved names and liveries disappeared as the white National corporate image took over from the individual liveries of former THC and BET fleets. The increase in car ownership and

Front cover: Rhondda Transport Co, 360, a Leyland PSUC/2 with Weymann bodywork, new in 1958 turns into the bus station at Bridgend in June 1963. The doors are open suggesting a warm day, it's passengers perhaps contemplating a day out in Porthcawl, the coach's probable destination. *Philip Wallis*

Back cover: An operator still trading today is Pulham's Bourton-on-the-Water, in Gloucestershire. Twenty-five years ago, Plaxton-bodied Leyland PSU3, HDF 700L, was pictured in Moreton-in-Marsh on a stage journey in April 1975. *John Jones*

Title page: Perhaps a typical 1960s independent line-up, these Bedfords of Jones, Llanidloes, were actually photographed in February 1979. It comprises, left to right, an SB with Duple Super Vega bodywork, an older SB with Plaxton Consort body plus two long-serving Duple Vista-bodied OBs, by then almost 30 years old. *Tony Moyes*

First published 2001

ISBN 0 7110 2785 4

Published by Ian Allan Publishing

an imprint of Ian Allan Publishing Ltd, Hersham, Surrey KT12 4RG.
Printed by Ian Allan Printing Ltd, Hersham, Surrey KT12 4RG.

Code: 0104/B2

Shipping operator David MacBrayne began bus operation as far back as 1906 and continued until the takeover by the Scottish Bus Group in 1969. Operations were gradually transferred over to Highland Omnibuses and Western SMT in stages during 1970-2. 186 (610 CYS) was a little 21-seat Duple-bodied Bedford C5C1 new in 1961, and was part of the last takeover, that of the services on Islay in January 1972. It is seen at Port Ellen in August 1970, some four months after the transfer of the first batch of services, around Inverness. 186 became Highland C29 but was soon disposed of, to begin some years of non-PSV use. *Chris Lodington*

cheap overseas package holidays were two factors in the general decline in coach travel as the 1970s progressed. 1980 saw the new Transport Act sweeping away licensing restrictions that had been in place for 50 years, while the deregulation of the bus industry in 1986 indirectly resulted in the demise of some well-known names in coaching.

The variety of coaching operators as featured in this book can be quite broad. We have all heard of the larger concerns, such as Barton, Grey-Green, Royal Blue and Wallace Arnold. Those that offer nationwide tour programmes can turn up almost anywhere in the country. There are also hundreds of small, very localised, one- or two-vehicle operators. Thumbing through the pages of the various fleetlists published over the years by the PSV Circle, one is struck by the sheer number of firms, perhaps village-based, with only a couple of vehicles to their name at any one time.

Work might consist of a school contract in the morning, a market-day run during the day to return to fulfil the school contract in the afternoon. In the evening, a tour might have been arranged, or a private-hire job to a darts match. Saturday might be taken up by a return journey to a nearby market town, while a trip to the seaside might occupy them on the Sunday. These were essentially local operators and as such were rarely seen far away from their home base. It follows therefore that their activities would generally be recorded only by local enthusiasts. Gathering together the illustrations for this book (and taking and collecting bus and coach photographs generally), I am struck that some small operators receive extensive coverage of their operations, while others are virtually unheard of. To my shame, a few of the following operators were totally unknown to me and required much searching through old fleetlists to find anything at all about them! I was certainly guilty of ignoring local coach operators when I began taking pictures in the 1970s — why waste film on yet another Duple-bodied Bedford? I now know better!

The following is therefore a rambling tour around the UK and

Ireland, stopping off here and there to sample the local operator. We begin in Scotland and progress to Ireland via the North East, North West, Yorkshire, the Midlands, East Anglia, London and the South East, the South West and Jersey, and South Wales.

Thanks are due to photographers who answered my call for pictures and indeed had the foresight not only to photograph coaches, but in colour also. I know for some of them in the 1960s it was a case of black and white or colour, as only one camera was owned! Thanks also to those of you who have offered snippets of information that have saved hours of research, in particular to Alan Munroe and Peter Tulloch. Acknowledgement is also made to the publications of the PSV Circle, without which this book would have been impossible to complete. Thanks too (or should it be sympathy?) to Maureen, my wife, now celebrating 21 years of my writing books, and threatening to open her own transport bookshop. Where will she get the stock, I wonder?

Kevin Lane
Dunstable
November 2000

Left: Other ex-MacBrayne vehicles did serve longer with Highland, including this Bedford SB5/Plaxton, wearing its new owner's colours and now numbered CD82. It had been acquired in November 1971 with operations on Mull, where it is probably seen during the mid-1970s. Withdrawal came in 1979, when the vehicle passed to Peace, Kirkwall. *Kevin Lane collection*

Above: MacBrayne's 1952 intake consisted of 22 Duple-bodied Bedford OLAZs, numbered 150-171. 163 (KGD 904), a 20-seater with space for a mail compartment, passed to Argyll operator McLachlan, Tayvallich, in 1967, and is seen here outside the little depot in 1970. This vehicle was later preserved, as was another of the batch, 162 (KGD 903). *Peter Tulloch*

Above right: 367 CKA was a Foden PVRF6 originally used by Fodens as a test vehicle and was built in 1951. It received a Plaxton Panorama body, modified to accommodate the rear engine, in 1959, when it was first registered. Its first owner was Topping's of Liverpool, later heading to the North East of Scotland with Bean's of Brechin, with whom it is seen here in 1970. Sadly it ended up with a dealer and later disappeared without trace. *Peter Tulloch*

Above: J. & J. Leith Ltd, operating from Nithsdale Garage, Sanquhar, in Dumfries & Galloway, bought KSM 40, a Santus-bodied Crossley SD42/7, in 1949. As with many of the smaller bodybuilders, the quality of construction was poor, and this necessitated a drastic rebuild, with all of the body, with the exception of the cab area, removed and replaced with an Alexander body from a Leyland Cheetah. Alongside KSM 40, seen here probably in the late 1960s, is another rebuilt vehicle, ex-Trent RC 9687, a 1947 AEC Regal I originally bodied by Willowbrook (B35F) but rebuilt with a full-front (FDP39F) in 1958. *Peter Tulloch*

Right: The 14-vehicle fleet of long-established operator Stark's Motor Services of Dunbar was taken over by Scottish Omnibuses at the beginning of 1964. The good name of the company was such that a number of Scottish Omnibuses' own vehicles received Stark's fleetname and livery. Alexander-bodied AEC Reliances B905-8, new in 1962, were among these, repainted in 1967; B906 is seen in Dunbar in the late 1960s. The 'S' suffix to the stock number is the garage code, in this case Dunbar (Starks). *Mike A. Sutcliffe*

BANK OF SCOTLAND
DUNBAR
B. WARD.
Newsagent & Tobacco
PLAYER'S cigarettes
BRISTOL
Kensitas
Stark's
YWS 906
UGG 81

Left: Bannatyne Motors began with a route on the Isle of Arran, acquired from Ribbeck's Motors, in April 1952. Further routes were added, but within 21 years Bannatyne had been taken over by the Arran Transport & Trading Co, this taking place in September 1973. Two Foden coaches have worked on Arran: Lennox's CSD 711, a Brockhouse-bodied PVSC6 which had been new to Hunter, Dreghorn (part of A1 Service), and Bannatyne's CCS 61, another PVSC6, this time with Scottish Aviation bodywork. This had also served with Hunter, although it had started life as a demonstrator for Scottish Aviation in 1947. Seen here at the garage at Blackfoot in June 1971, CCS 61 had, by this time, acquired a set of bus seats, with the exception of the five on the back row (presumably to keep any courting couples comfortable). Preservation was sadly denied CCS 61 and it went for scrap. *Peter Tulloch*

Over the years, Edinburgh Corporation has operated on its city tours, a varied coach fleet which has worn a striking black and white livery since 1955. The first postwar coaches were Bedford OBs in 1949/50, and Bedfords were again favoured, although not exclusively, during the 1960s/70s and after the transfer of the fleet to Lothian Region Transport in 1975. Five Bedford coaches were taken into stock in 1969 — two VALs and three VAMs, all Duple-bodied, including PSC 232G, seen at Waverley station when new, with an earlier Bedford SB5 behind. *Mike A. Sutcliffe*

Above: The history of United Automobile's coach services between the North East of England and London goes back to the 1930s. Before this, services were in the hands of a number of independent operators, including Armstrong of Ebchester, trading as Majestic, and Orange of Bedlington, which had pioneered services back in 1926. Within 10 years, all competition had sold out to United, giving it a monopoly of services between Tyneside, Teesside and London. Orange's influence was long-lived, however; the Orange fleetname survived until the 1950s, whilst the olive green and cream livery continued in use until National Bus Company days.

The circus is in town, as United UE704 (904 THN), a 1963 ECW-bodied Bristol MW6G, leaves an overcast Doncaster to head south in the late 1960s, on a service 205 journey from Newcastle via Teesside and York. *Mike A. Sutcliffe*

Right: Doncaster again, although on a rather brighter day this time. OK Motor Services Plaxton-bodied AEC Reliance 5050 PT was only a month old when caught on hire to Hall Bros, working from Tyneside to Nottingham in September 1961. Hall Bros, of South Shields, had worked from Newcastle to Doncaster since 1930 (and, later, Coventry), and continued to do so until it sold out to Barton in 1967. One of the firm's own coaches, Bedford SB ECU 927, is alongside. OK Motor Services was perhaps better known for its bus services around Bishop Auckland, and was acquired by Go-Ahead Group in 1995. As for 5050 PT, it passed to Howe of Spennymoor in 1970 and back to OK two years later, finally leaving the fleet in 1974. *Roger Holmes*

FRUIT
OWERS
BRAMHAMS
Furniture
Showrooms
YER'S cigarettes
PLAYER'S
ON HIRE TO
HALL BROS.
NOTTINGHAM
"OK"
PRIVATE
OK MOTOR SERVICES
5050 PT
HALL
ECU 92

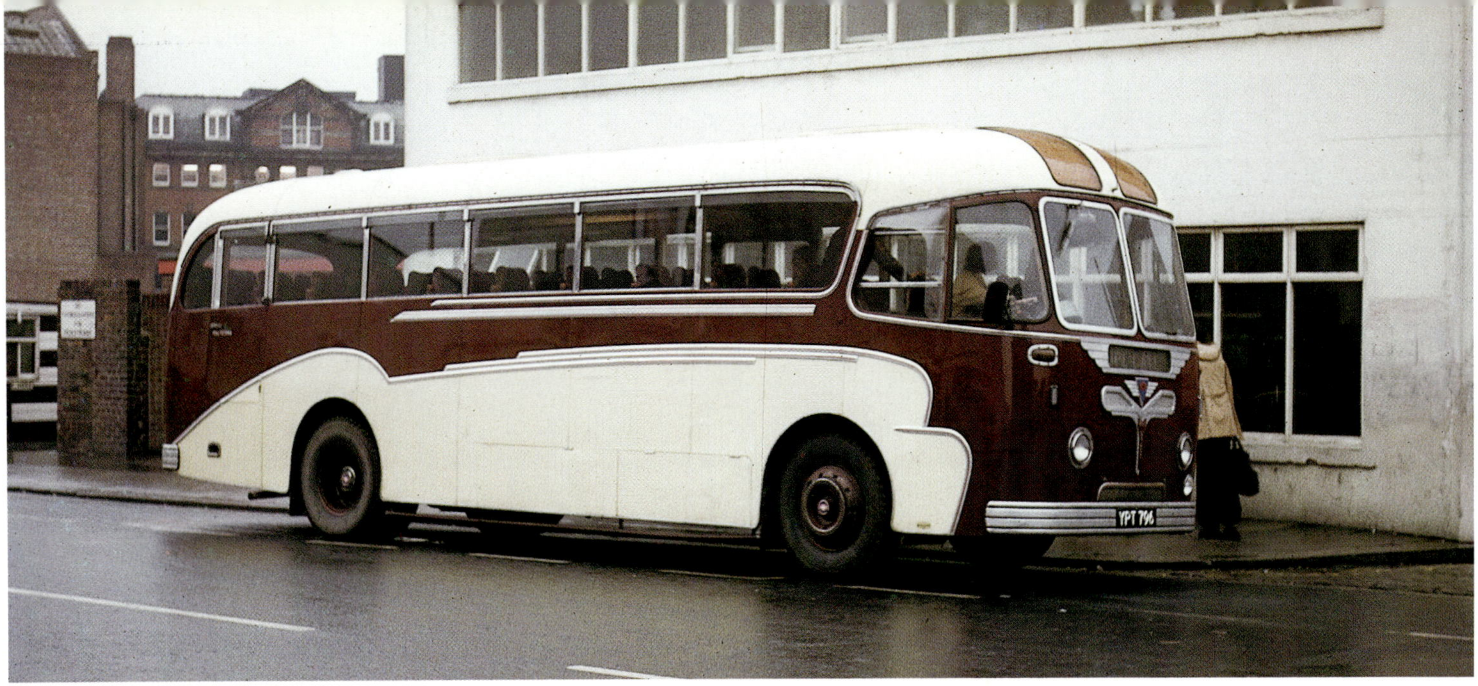
YPT 796

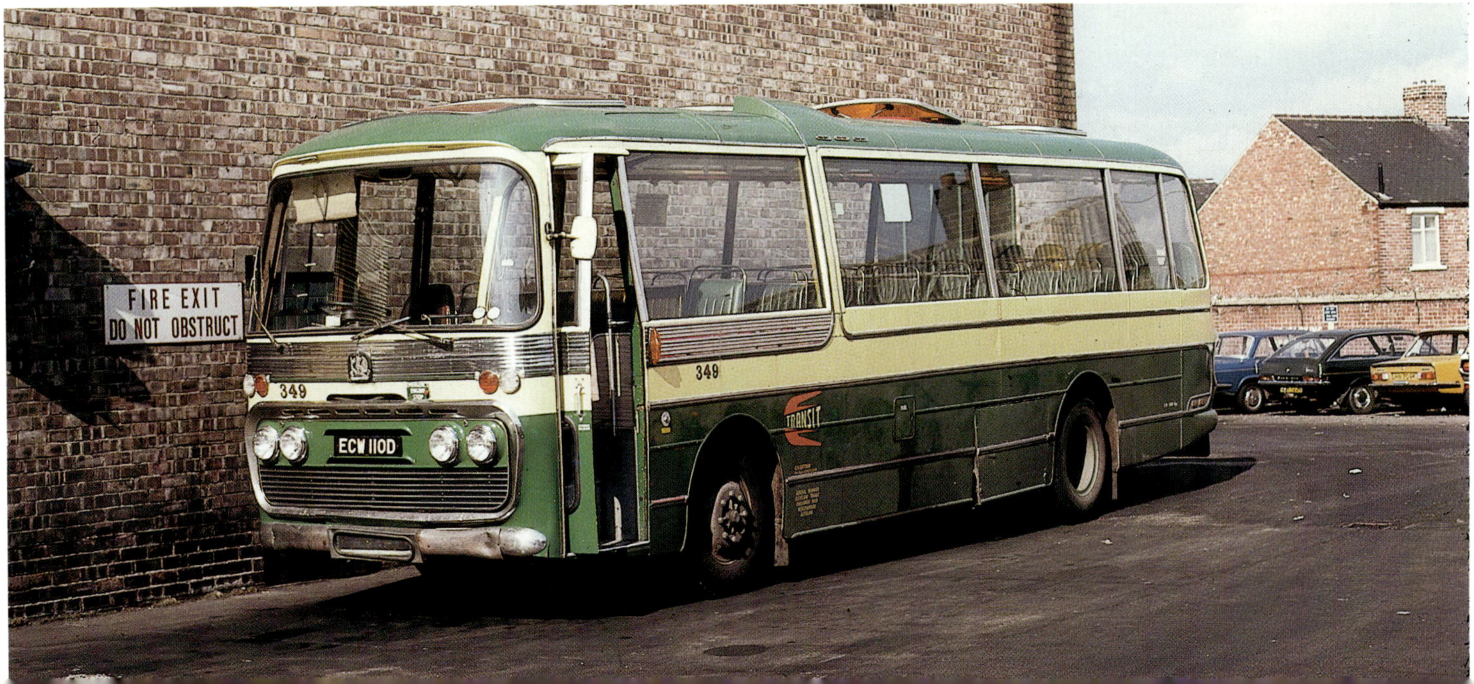
FIRE EXIT
DO NOT OBSTRUCT
349
ECW 110D
349
TRANSIT

Left: G. R. Anderson and E. W. Wilson were jointly responsible for the Economic Bus Service of Whitburn. Although formerly a partnership, they later formed separate companies. The service between Sunderland and Whitburn was taken over by the Tyne & Wear PTE in April 1975. Wilson contributed a dozen vehicles, including YPT 796, a Roe-bodied AEC Reliance supplied new in 1958; it is seen in Sunderland six months before the takeover. All 12 vehicles soon passed to a dealer, YPT 796 ending up as a caravan. *John Jones*

Below left: North Yorkshire independent operator Saltburn Motor Services dated back to 1928. Local services around Saltburn-on-Sea were operated, as well as a number of works and contract services serving industrial Teesside. In addition, an express service was run from Loftus to Blackpool on summer Sundays. More unusually, a 15in-gauge miniature railway was also operated in Saltburn! Bus operations were acquired by Cleveland Transit in 1974, rolling stock comprising mainly Bedford coaches. One such was Bedford VAM/Duple ECW 110D, new in 1966 to Lancashire operator Tattersall, Padiham, and arriving in Saltburn via Central Motors, Burnley, in 1969. It subsequently became Cleveland Transit S349. By the time that it was photographed behind Middlesbrough garage in September 1981, it had acquired bus seats, with the exception of those in the back row. Withdrawal came in 1982. *Kevin Lane*

Below: There were countless Bedford SBs running in the North East of England from the 1950s to the 1970s, operators in the area being very loyal to the model. Illustrated is CPT 272B, carrying a Duple Firefly body, of Fir Tree Coaches, Crook, in County Durham. The coach is pictured in Bishop Auckland in June 1977, passing an AEC Reliance of Bond Bros, Willington. *John Jones*

ADC 195B
PRIVATE
BUP 396B
PRIVATE CHARTER
PRIMROSE
53 JPT
2002 BT

PRIVATE
CUMBERLAND
LAO 581E

Above left: A trio of Bedfords on a sunny June day in 1965. ADC 195B is a VAL14 with N&R, Elsecar, newly-acquired from Begg, Thornaby, to whom it was new a year previously. Of a similar vintage is BUP 396B of Primrose, Winlanton Mill, and from the same fleet is AEC Reliance/Plaxton 53 JPT. *Michael Fowler*

Left: Few major operators got their hands on the Bedford VAL, although notable exceptions included Southern Vectis, Hants & Dorset and Manchester City Transport. Cumberland Motor Services bought four new Duple-bodied examples in 1965-7, and numbered them 1300-3. 1303 is seen on hire to Ribble on its way to Blackpool c1970. *Mike A. Sutcliffe*

Above: Blackpool is undoubtedly the most popular coaching destination in the North West of England, and much film must have been exposed photographing visiting vehicles over the years. Two Bedfords sit side by side, probably in the late 1960s; centre-stage is 4220 TE, one of a pair of VAL14s delivered to Robinson, Great Harwood, in 1963. This particular coach ended up rather further away than Blackpool, being exported to Sri Lanka in 1981. The other Bedford, 181 WTJ, is a Yeates Fiesta-bodied SB1 new to Bracewell, Colne, in 1961. *Peter Tulloch*

Above: Of the northwestern coach operators no longer with us, it is perhaps Rochdale-based Yelloway that is most lamented. The company was formed c1930 from another coach operator, Holt's of Bacup, and grew steadily with a network of, in the main, express coach services between Lancashire and other parts of the UK. Yelloway was sold to dealer Carlton PSV in July 1985, which in turn became part of the ATL group. Many problems lay ahead, and by the end of the decade the Yelloway name had disappeared — a sad loss.

The AEC was a feature of the fleet for many years, and in 1978, when PDK 459H was seen leaving Ashton-under-Lyne on the X49 Glossop-Fleetwood service, the fleet was composed almost entirely of Reliances with Plaxton bodywork, the exceptions being two with Duple bodies. With the demise of AEC, the company turned to the Leyland Leopard and Tiger. *Roger Holmes*

Right: Yelloway's image was distinctive; this board advertising the company's express service to South West England was photographed at Knutsford bus station, Cheshire, in June 1977. *Tony Moyes*

North Western Road Car took delivery of 30 Leyland Tiger Cubs with Willowbrook bodies in 1959/60 — the last of this chassis for the operator. All were intended as dual-purpose vehicles, although a shortage of coaches at the time saw 10 fitted with coach seats. One of these, 773 (LDB 773) is seen in later life, demoted to bus work — in this instance, Macclesfield local route 58. On the break-up of the company in 1972, 773 passed to Crosville. *Photobus*

NORTH WESTERN
SCARBOROUGH
X25
NORTH WESTERN
256
KJA256F

Left: North Western's 1968 intake of coaches totalled 15 vehicles, all Leyland Leopards. Ten were bodied by Alexander and five by Duple. The five Duple Commanders were numbered 255-9; 256, KJA 256F, is seen when probably only a year or so old, setting off on an X25 journey from Northwich to (hopefully) sunny Scarborough. The batch passed to National Travel North West in 1972. *Photobus*

Right: Crosville, along with many other National Bus Company subsidiaries, operated a few non-standard coaches, in this case Bedford VAMs. Two batches were bought, in 1967 and 1969; CVF691 (XFM 691G) was the first of four Duple-bodied VAM70s delivered in 1969, and is seen crunching over slate at Llanberis in June 1974. *Chris Lodington*

Above: A number of Bedford VALs ran on the Isle of Man, all second-hand vehicles from mainland UK. Duple-bodied VAL14 NMN 111 of Tours (Isle of Man) Ltd was originally JAX 898D, new to Jones, Aberbeeg, in 1966. It also carries the name of Corkill's, the main constituent of Tours, and is seen in Douglas. *Kevin Lane collection*

Right: Many well-known names in coaching are but a memory. One still at the forefront, however, is Leeds-based Wallace Arnold Tours. Wallace Cunningham and Arnold Crowe had been operating since 1912, continuing until taken over by haulage/charabanc operator Robert Barr of Leeds in 1926. From 1933, expansion saw the acquisition of many other operators, mainly in Yorkshire, but including several in Devon, and London-based Evan Evans. One of those in Yorkshire was Feather Brother (Tours) Ltd of Bradford, taken over in 1955 and duly becoming a subsidiary. Carrying both Feathers Tours and Wallace Arnold identities, 216 HUM, one of 17 Leyland Leopard PSU3/3Rs delivered in 1964 with centre-entrance Plaxton Embassy bodies, proceeds through Leicester later in the decade. *Mike A. Sutcliffe*

VIP
FEATHERS
TOURS
Wallace Arnold
216 HUM
DJF 440C

Left: Another well-known West Yorkshire independent was Samuel Ledgard of Otley, which also had a long history, stretching back to before World War 1. Always an interesting fleet, perhaps better known for the many elderly buses operated, it also contained a number of notable coaches.

Along with GBU 537, GBU 539 was acquired from Broadway Motors, Hollinwood, in 1960. They were Plaxton-bodied Leyland Tiger PS2/3s new in 1951, and lasted until 1963. Plans to rebuild the chassis to Leyland PD2/37 specification and rebody them as double-deckers were not completed, and both chassis went for scrap in 1967. Samuel Ledgard was eventually bought out by West Yorkshire Road Car in 1967, only a handful of vehicles seeing further service with the latter. *Photobus*

Left: West Riding Automobile Co was unusual amongst the larger company operators in managing to remain independent for many years. In 1967 it sold out to the Transport Holding Co and thence passed to the National Bus Company. A mixed coaching fleet was running during the 1960s; in June 1965, for example, it ranged from Leyland Tiger PS2s through to Bedford VALs and SB5s. This particular view dates from a little earlier, October 1964, at Castleford, and depicts CHL 274, a 1950 AEC Regal III with a Longford C33F body, alongside Roe bus-bodied Leyland Tiger PS2 EHL 337. CHL 274, numbered 333, was withdrawn in 1965. *Michael Fowler*

Above: United Services was Yorkshire's last bus-operating co-operative, and Bingley of Kinsley was the last member. It took over Cooper of South Kirkby in April 1977, only to succumb itself to the West Yorkshire PTE later in the same month. Back in 1964 Bingley took delivery of BWX 597B, a Duple Northern-bodied Leyland Leopard PSU3/3RT, seen on its way to Wakefield c1965. *Mike A. Sutcliffe*

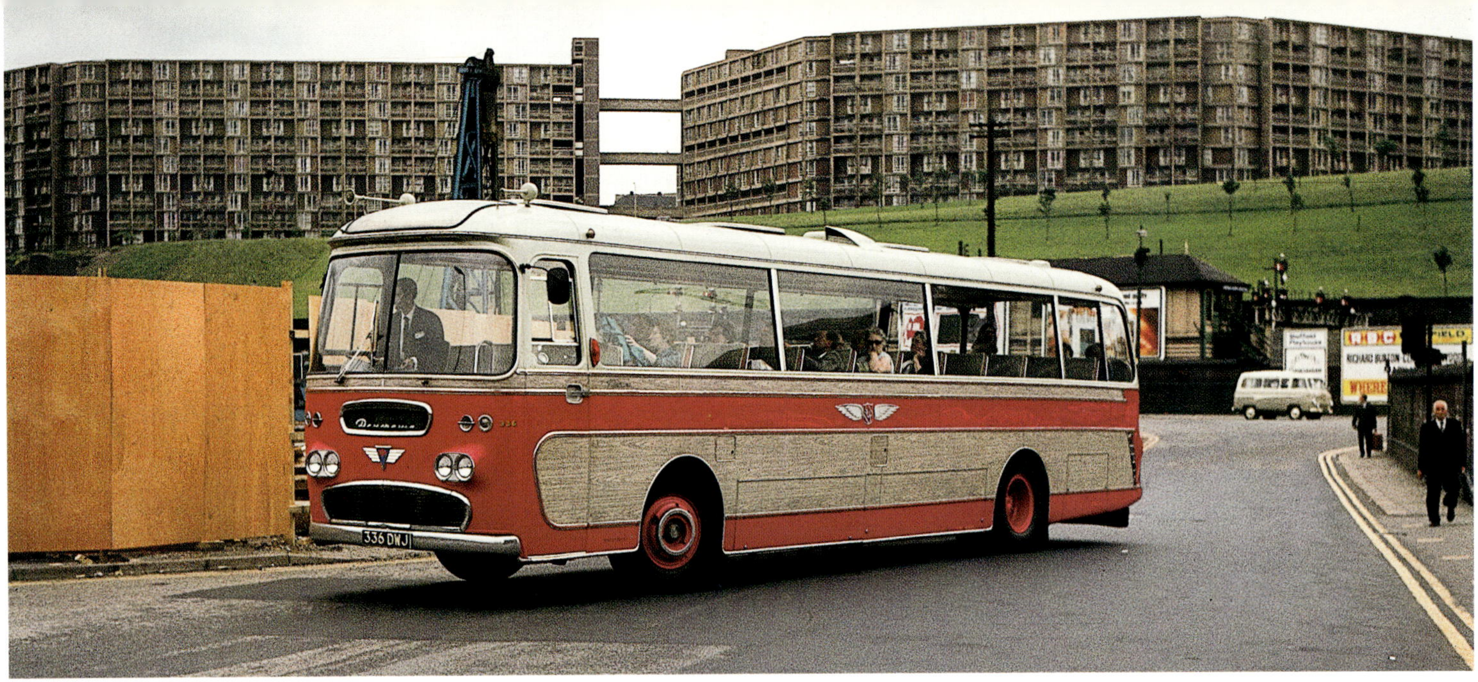
336 DWJ

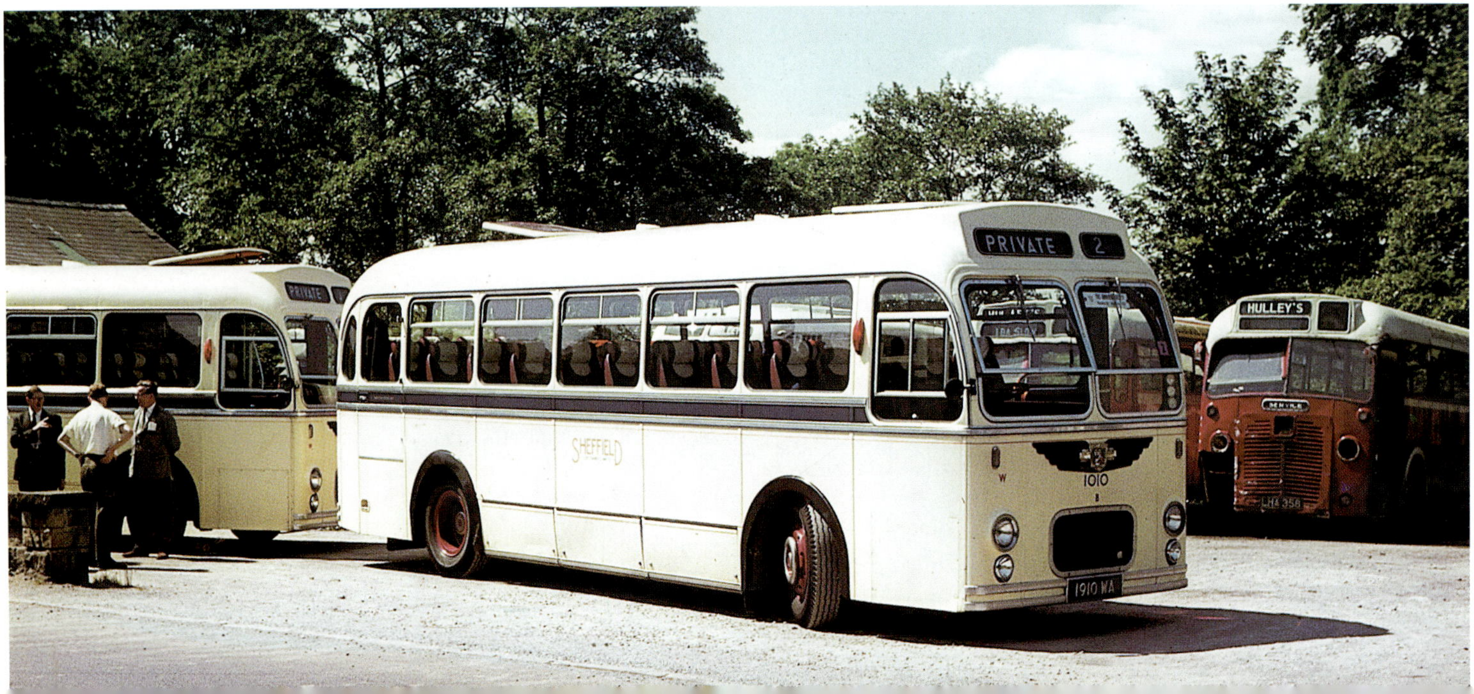
PRIVATE
2
SHEFFIELD
1010
1910 WA
HULLEY'S
LHA 358

Left: The origins of Sheffield United Tours date back to 1926, with a company formed as Arthur Kitson Ltd. 1935 saw a joint takeover by North Western Road Car, East Midland Motor Services and Yorkshire Traction and a change of name to Sheffield United Tours Ltd. In 1974 SUT and Hebble were merged to form National Travel (North East) Ltd.

336 (336 DWJ) was a Plaxton-bodied AEC Reliance new in 1962, seen here passing construction work at Pond Street bus station, Sheffield, in the 1960s; Sheffield Midland station and the flats rising above form the backdrop. 336 DWJ duly passed to NT(NE) in 1974, albeit in a withdrawn state, being subsequently stripped for spares. *Mike A. Sutcliffe*

Left: A curious situation existed in Sheffield where the Corporation ran three fleets: the 'A' fleet was Corporation-owned, the 'B' fleet was owned jointly between the Corporation and British Railways (as successors to the LMSR and LNER, which had transferred their bus services in 1929), and the 'C' fleet was owned wholly by British Railways. Two Leyland Leopard L1s were delivered to the 'B' fleet in 1961, fitted with ECW 41-seat bodies – a rare combination. Both are seen here on an enthusiasts' tour at the premises of Hulley of Baslow, Derbyshire, in the late 1960s. *Mike A. Sutcliffe*

Above: Booth & Fisher, situated on the Derbyshire/South Yorkshire borders, began operating after World War 1, building up a strong local following. Its bus-buying came in phases, and from the late 1930s and into the 1950s, Bedfords were in favour. LRB 749 was a Barnaby-bodied OB, new in 1948 seen here enjoying a day at Doncaster Races in September 1962. It was sold for use as a mobile shop in 1965. Sister vehicle LRB 750 enjoyed a happier fate, ending up in preservation. Booth & Fisher survived until swallowed up by South Yorkshire PTE in 1976. *Michael Fowler*

PRIVATE
17
17
DUPLE
SNN 458F

Left: At a time when coaches in municipal service were rare, Chesterfield Corporation was unusual in its acquisition of Duple Viceroy-bodied Bedford VAM70 SNN 458F from Nottinghamshire independent Lindrick of Langold in 1970. Carrying fleetnumber 17, it is seen on a private-hire journey at Shrewsbury in August 1975. *John Jones*

Above: The little representation of the cartoon cat Felix has adorned the vehicles of Norman Frost for some years. He first ran a Crossley as a coal lorry during the week and as a charabanc at weekends (try doing *that* today!) as far back as 1921. For the past 70 years, his main service has been that between Derby and Ilkeston, on which service Yeates Europa-bodied Bedford SB 3 XRA is seen during the late 1960s. *Mike A. Sutcliffe*

Above: There can be few bus enthusiasts who have not heard of Barton Transport. Not only was it one of the largest independent operators in the country, but it was also among the oldest, going way back to 1900. Most too will know of the great variety of rolling stock running during the 1950s and '60s, and be aware of the seemingly indecent elimination of all double-deckers and secondhand vehicles from the fleet in the early 1970s.

Many operators have been taken over during the lifetime of the company, including eight during the 1960s, that of Hall Bros, South Shields, being mentioned earlier in this book. February 1961 saw the acquisition of Cream Bus Service, Stamford, a fleet including 15 Bedford coaches. One of these was ECT 190, a Duple-bodied OB new in 1949. It is seen here with Barton fleetnames, probably soon after takeover, as it was disposed of early in 1962. Perhaps more interesting is the coach alongside, Windover-bodied AEC Regal III DJD 152. New in 1950 to Clarke's Luxury Coaches, London, it was acquired by Cream in 1955. Like the OB, it didn't last long with Barton, being soon withdrawn and scrapped. *Mike A. Sutcliffe*

Right: In May 1966 Barton took over Provincial Garage (Leicester) Ltd. A dozen coaches, all bought new, were acquired, most lasting into the 1970s. Two of its AEC Reliances are seen here at the garage wearing a mixture of identities; XBC 546 (Barton 1055) was new in 1960 and carries Duple bodywork, while Plaxton-bodied 45 DJF (Barton 1058) was new in 1962. Both would remain in the fleet until 1974. *Mike A. Sutcliffe*

PROVINCIAL
R15
LEICESTER
1055
1055
BARTON
XBC 546
PROVINCIAL
Provincial Panorama
BARTON
45 DJF

SOUTH NOTTS
KINGSTON
KINGSTON SHOW
KINGSTON SHOW
63
SOUTH NOTTS
LOE 900

Left: Another well-known Nottinghamshire independent operator was South Notts Bus Co, based at Gotham, between Nottingham and Loughborough. The company, in which Barton had a 50% stake, could trace its origins back to 1928. With its operation of double-deckers, and including a busy route worked jointly with two neighbouring municipals, South Notts always had a 'big company' feel about it. Coaches have also featured in the fleet, including a pair of 1951 Leyland Royal Tigers with Duple Roadmaster bodies, both new to Jackson, Castle Bromwich, and acquired in 1957. LOE 900, looking rather down at heel, sits in the sun at the Kingston Show in August 1964. South Notts was taken over by Nottingham City Transport in 1991, although livery and name have both been retained. *Roger Holmes*

Right: Yet another independent in the county of Nottinghamshire with a wider following was Gash of Newark, perhaps better known for its use of elderly Daimler double-deckers. W. W. Gash was another early operator, charging passengers to travel in his horse and cart from Elston to Newark in 1919. Jumping forward to the 1980s, deregulation saw competition with Lincolnshire Road Car in Newark, which included the use of Routemasters, but Gash eventually sold out to its rival in 1989.

Coaches bought over the years have included Daimlers and a fair few Bedfords, while, more recently, Bristol LHs and Leyland Leopards have been favoured. SCH 636R is a Leyland Leopard PSU3E/4R with a 51-seat Plaxton body, new in 1977, seen in Newark on its way to the bus station to take up service to Retford in April 1988. This vehicle duly passed to Road Car a year later, being numbered 1475.
Kevin Lane

WESLEY'S COACHES
WESLEY'S
WESLEYS
372 BBH
8 DAY DEVON &
CORNWALL TOUR

Left: Wesley, Stoke Goldington, Northamptonshire, had origins dating back to 1925 and a Ford T bus. Postwar, the company had a predilection for Crossleys and Commers, both bought in large numbers between 1948 and 1968, before moving on to Fords. Duple-bodied 372 BBH was the fourth Commer Avenger in the fleet, having been bought new in 1957 and lasting until acquired for preservation 15 years later. It is seen here in August 1961 at Land's End on a Devon & Cornwall Tour. *Roger Holmes*

Above: Coventry was another of those municipal operators to buy coaches before this became fashionable. In 1964 four coaches were added to the fleet, to join a trio of Daimler Freelines delivered in 1959. Three of the new arrivals were Duple-bodied Bedford SB5s, but the fourth was CDU 51B, a petrol-engined Thames Trader carrying a Martin Walter C25F body, bought to test its suitability for transporting disabled children. *Mike A. Sutcliffe*

Above: Midland Red's postwar coach production saw the development of the C class, from the C1 of 1949 through to the CM6Ts of the mid-1960s. By this time, the company was also turning to more standard vehicles from outside manufacturers. 1965 saw not only the arrival of the CM6Ts but also 49 Leyland Leopard PSU3/4R coaches with Duple Commander bodywork, designated LC7. 5787 waits to embark on what looks set to be a damp evening tour from Leicester, when nearly new. *Mike A. Sutcliffe*

Right: Stratford-upon-Avon Blue Motors — 'Stratford Blue' — was founded in 1927 and acquired by Midland Red in 1935. It was operated as a separate concern until fully absorbed in 1971, although the name would re-surface after deregulation. A small coaching unit was operated, and, as with the bus fleet, Leylands were favoured. The first Leyland Leopard, 436 GAC, was a PSU3/3R fitted with Duple Alpine Continental 49-seat bodywork and new in 1963. Numbered 55, it is seen at Stratford during the late 1960s. *Mike A. Sutcliffe*

519
STRATFORD
Stratford Blue
55
436 GAC

Above: It is perhaps appropriate that Wye Valley Motors should be represented here by a Bedford OB, a type that was bought in some numbers. They lasted a long time in the fleet, too; in 1970, *Buses* magazine reported that 16 of the type were still in stock in March of that year. Duple-bodied HCJ 152, seen in Hereford, was new in 1950 — the only one to be bought that year — and was photographed in August 1970. The last OBs were eventually ousted by Bedford SBs. *John Jones*

Right: South Midland came to Thames Valley from the Red & White group when the latter was nationalised in 1950. Most of the fleet built up during the 1950s and '60s was a traditional combination of Bristol and ECW, although Bedfords were also favoured. Decidedly non-standard, however, was 85, SFC 571, an AEC Regal IV with ECW bodywork, and not a Bristol LS as one might think. Eleven years old in 1963, it is seen at Oxford, waiting to load for London. Considering the vehicles currently plying between the two cities, the livery is decidedly restrained! *Philip Wallis*

SOUTH MIDLAND
SOUTH MIDLAND
SFC 571

British Rail Reading General
THAMES VALLEY
POLICE NO PARKING
POLICE NO PARKING
RJB 426F

Left: In 1967, Thames Valley was granted a licence to operate a service between Reading General station and London Heathrow Airport. This replaced a service previously operated from Slough to Heathrow by Rickards Coaches. C426, RJB 426F, is one of a quartet of Duple Commander-bodied Bristol RELH6Gs delivered in 1968, replacing Bedfords on the Heathrow run, and is seen at Reading when fairly new. *Mike A. Sutcliffe*

Above: The City of Oxford coaching fleet was quite modest, until the South Midland operations of Thames Valley were transferred in 1971. This was all well in the future when six AEC Regal IVs with Willowbrook C37C bodies were delivered in 1952, including SFC 607, on layover, possibly in London. *Mike A. Sutcliffe*

OXFORD-CAMBRIDGE
EXPRESS
SERVICE
OXFORD
DAD 430K
Bus Stop
UNITED COUNTIES

Left: Service 39, between Oxford and Cambridge, was a joint operation between Premier Travel, Cambridge, and Percival's Motors, Oxford. Three daily journeys each way were run, taking five minutes under three hours to complete, via Aylesbury and Luton. Percival's DAD 430K was a Bedford YRQ/Plaxton, new to Luxury, Stow-on-the-Wold, in August 1972, and is working the 14.15 from Cambridge through Dunstable on a Sunday afternoon in August 1981. The current National Express service 347 between Great Yarmouth and Plymouth incorporates the 39, but frequency is down to one journey a day, each way, thus eliminating the prospect of a day in either Oxford or Cambridge from Dunstable! *Kevin Lane*

Above: Smith's Luxury Coaches (Reading) Ltd was a large independent, perhaps best known to the enthusiast for its interesting fleet of double-deckers, once operated on contract duties, principally to AERE, Harwell, and AWRE, Aldermaston. A coach fleet was used extensively on tours and excursions, while repairs and overhauls were also undertaken for other small operators. The mid-1960s saw the replacement by Bedford SBs of a number of Dennis Lancets. This view, therefore, taken in July 1963, illustrates the transition, although this particular Duple-bodied SB, MDP 352, was new in 1956. Dennis Lancet J3 EDP 818 also carries a Duple body, and was new in 1950. *Philip Wallis*

Another large Berkshire independent, this time one still with us, is Reliance Motor Services, Newbury. Like Smith's, it also undertook contract services to Harwell and Aldermaston, as well as tours, excursions, etc. Two Duple-bodied Bedford SBs, XBK 40 and DRX 747C, are seen here at Newbury c1966, perhaps preparing to depart on a local tour. *Mike A. Sutcliffe*

Also still trading is Charlton Services, based in the attractive Oxfordshire village of Charlton-on-Otmoor. The first service into Oxford dates back to the 1920s, run by Charlton's predecessor, Forget-Me-Not Coaches, the present company taking over in 1955. In May 1963, Leyland Tiger Cub/Duple 332 BHA loads at Oxford. The vehicle was new to the Gliderways, Smethwick, fleet. On the right is United Counties Bristol MW6G/ECW 142, WBD 142, loading on service 121, before embarking on the two-hour run to Bletchley. This was a joint operation with City of Oxford. *Mike A. Sutcliffe*

BUCKMASTER
25 MTN
BUCKMASTER COACHES
EXPRESS & EXCURSION
SERVICES
PRIVATE HIRE COACHES
LEIGHTON BUZZARD 2743
BLETCHLEY 2952
23 JTM

Left: A bit of self-indulgence here! I grew up in Leighton Buzzard during the 1960s, and although I wasn't particularly interested in buses — it was all trains then — I do remember Buckmaster Coaches and its garage in North Street. These memories are of ex-London Transport RTLs, one of which took us on a school trip to Tring Museum; such was the noise we made upstairs that the driver threatened to have us ejected in case we came through into his cab! But I digress. Two Bedfords sit in the yard: Plaxton-bodied VAL14 25 MTM, half of a pair bought new in 1964, and Duple-bodied SB 23 JTM. *Mike A. Sutcliffe*

Above: Eagle, of Castle Acre, near Swaffham, in Norfolk, owned this Churchill-bodied Commer Avenger I, NNG 777, seen on the operator's stage service from Kings Lynn in January 1974. *Tony Moyes*

Bristol
OHY 998
105 MYD
CULLINGS
BRISTOL
OHY 990

Left: Although Bristol had introduced the LS model to succeed the L in 1952, Bristol Tramways ordered 10 LWLs with 'Queen Mary'-style ECW bodies for delivery in that year. (The only later LWLs went to Wilts & Dorset.) In 1965, several of Bristol's, including OHY 998 and OHY 990, passed to Culling, of Claxton, in Norfolk, where they are seen in August 1969. *Geoff Mills*

Above: AEC Reliances with Alexander bodies were bought regularly by Premier Travel, Cambridge. They arrived in pairs most years between 1964 and 1974, although four came in the latter year, to total 20 vehicles in all. OVE 232J, one of the two delivered in 1971, is seen at Cheltenham in July 1976 working an 'Eastlander' journey from Felixstowe, a jointly-operated service started in 1966. *John Jones*

STRATFORD ON-AVON
CAMBRIDGE
PROGRESSIVE
PROGRESSIVE
KDD 279E

Left: Black & White Motorways bought 38 Daimler Roadliner coaches between 1966 and 1970. Poor reliability soon saw them off to pastures new; all had been withdrawn by 1975. The seven vehicles of the 1967 batch all went in 1971, two passing to Harris, Cambridge, where they stayed until 1974. KDD 279E is pictured at Waterbeach. *Geoff Mills*

Right: Vines, of Great Bromley, Essex, operated this 1947 Burlingham-bodied Dennis Lancet III, MPU 395, new to Victory, Romford. *Geoff Mills*

Below right: The shape of things to come: the first Kässbohrer Setra integral coach in the UK went to Kirbys, Rayleigh, Essex, in August 1971. The operator was sufficiently impressed to buy more of the type, even retaining OTW 116K, seen at the Brighton Coach Rally in 1972, in the fleet into 2000. *Geoff Mills*

Above: Galleon Tours was the name used by Galleon World Travel as the owner of Essex County Coaches of Stratford. The combination of AEC Reliance chassis and Plaxton bodywork was usual for many years. Here AYW 569H, one of a batch of five delivered new in 1970, is seen in Berwick-upon-Tweed on a Scottish tour in June 1978. Note the fleetname on the roof! *John Jones*

Right: By the 1970s the George Ewer Group had become one of the largest coach operators in the UK, having benefited from a number of takeovers, particularly in the 1950s and 1960s. Orange Luxury Coaches was one such acquisition, in 1953, remaining as a subsidiary until 1975. Back in 1966 it had been decided to use just two trading names — Grey-Green and Orange. Wearing Orange colours is Plaxton-bodied Leyland Leopard PSU3B/4R JRK 620K, one of a batch of 10 delivered in 1972, laying over at Colchester. The George Ewer Group itself was taken over by the Cowie Group in 1981, the Grey-Green name disappearing into Arriva in 1998. *Geoff Mills*

IPSWICH-FELIXSTOWE
RELIEF COACH
ORANGE
LEOPARD
ORANGE
JRK 620K

Left: Another of the Ewer Group takeovers was that of World Wide Coaches, Camberwell, acquired over the period 1974-6. Notable in this fleet of luxury coaches were a number of Mercedes-Benz 0302s bought in the early 1970s. GMC 746J is seen in use as a hotel courtesy coach at Heathrow Airport in August 1977. *Kevin Lane collection*

Left: National Travel (South East) was the result of the amalgamation of National Bus Company coaching operators Tilling's, Timpson's and Samuelson's in 1974. This was renamed National Travel (London) in 1979, although the Tilling's element had passed to Eastern National in 1978. Quite a mixed bag of chassis was inherited, including Leylands, Fords and AECs, while Tilling's, as might be expected, provided Bristols. After formation, some unusual vehicles were delivered, including a coach-seated Leyland National in 1975 and four left-hand-drive Willowbrook-bodied AEC Reliances in 1976. The latter were used on continental services and were licensed in this country only to operate between London and the Channel ports. OYT 531R is pictured inside the former Samuelson's garage at Victoria when still fairly new. *Kevin Lane collection*

Twenty-two vehicles entered the East Kent fleet in 1952, all coaches. Three of these were FFN 448-50, Park Royal-bodied Leyland PSU1 Royal Tigers, and were used on tour duties for the first five years. FFN 449 still appears to be in use as such in June 1963, operating for Leroy Tours, at Victoria Coach Station. East Kent certainly got its money's-worth from these vehicles, not withdrawing them until 1967/8. Alongside is year-old AEC Reliance/Park Royal 527 FN in Europabus livery. This entire batch of vehicles received new Plaxton bodies in 1972/3. *Philip Wallis*

Above: When Maidstone & District took over Scout Motor Co, Hastings, in 1951 and Skinner's Luxury Coaches, St Leonards, in 1953, such was the goodwill that their separate identities were retained into the 1960s. This was not generally an uncommon practice, although the actual vehicles taken over didn't always last long, often being non-standard types. Those from Scout had all gone by 1953, although the AEC Regals of Skinner's survived well into the 1960s. A few of the main M&D fleet were subsequently painted into Scout or Skinner's colours, including 4442 (442 LKE), a Harrington-bodied AEC Reliance, one of 20 delivered in 1960 and seen here in 1968. It arrived new in Skinner's colours and remained so adorned until 1969. It was withdrawn as 3203 in 1977, having been demoted to bus duties. *Mike A. Sutcliffe*

Right: An earlier Maidstone & District AEC Reliance/Harrington was 381 BKM, new in 1957 as CO381 and withdrawn as 4381 in 1970. It passed to Davie's Coaches (Rye) Ltd, in whose employment it is seen here. *Photobus/Arnold Richardson*

DAVIE'S of RYE
DAVIE'S of RYE
381 BKM
New

Above: Some early postwar Bristol Ls of Hants & Dorset carried bodywork other than ECW, including Beadle and Dutfield. Another supplier was Portsmouth Aviation, seen here on this L6G, 679, KEL 407, of 1950, looking a little dated at Bournemouth in 1961. *Mike A. Sutcliffe.*

Right: On the face of it, the Isle of Wight was an unlikely place to find the Bedford VAL, in view of the fact that Southern Vectis was a Tilling company. Southern Vectis itself took a dozen VALs, while two more came with Shamrock & Rambler's Isle of Wight interests in 1969. Many also found favour with independents on the island, such as West Wight Motors, Moss Motor Tours and Shotters of Brightstone. Illustrated is Southern Vectis 404 (EDL 993D), a Duple-bodied VAL14, new in 1966 and seen at Ryde on a bright spring morning in 1975. Like many VALs, it ended its days as a non-PSV, in this case as a caravan. *John Jones*

SOUTHERN VECTIS
DUPLE
EDL 993D
PRIVATE
BUNGALOWS COTTAGES
HOTELS & GUEST HOUSES
WAY RIDDETT
TOWN HALL CHAMBERS
RYDE
AUCTIONS
FURNITURE

Above: The Associated Motorways network initially involved six operators — Black & White Motorways, Bristol, Midland Red, Red & White Services, Royal Blue and United Counties — and as such their vehicles were a common sight on the roads of Britain until services were transferred to National Travel in 1973. Black & White 227 (6777 DD) was one of nine Plaxton-bodied Leyland Leopards delivered in 1962. It is seen amongst City of Oxford AEC Regents at Gloucester Green in September 1963, working between Cheltenham and London. Ten years later 6777 DD was withdrawn and passed to a contractor. *Philip Wallis*

Right: Inevitably, duplication was required at peak times on Associated Motorways services, and this could involve operators outside of the usual pool. Perrett, Shipton Oliffe, bought three Bedford SB5/Duple Super Vegas in 1962, one of which, 5329 DD, is seen on such a duty at Cheltenham in May 1969. Note the wonderful period posters on the adjacent wall, and the line-up of Black & White coaches in the background. *Colin Martin*

WESTON s MARE
STONEHOUSE
CAMBRIDGE
FILTON
BRISTOL
BACKWELL
CONGRESBURY
CLACTON-ON-SEA
BEDFORD
Super Vega
5329 DD
PERRETT'S

Above: From 1948, several Bristol-area independents were combined to form Wessex Coaches Ltd. Further acquisitions followed, from Bristol and Somerset, and subsidiary companies were formed. A contract fleet was also operated at various power station sites from 1958, the latter using both buses and coaches. The various companies were eventually absorbed into National Travel (South West) between 1974 and 1976. For many years, new purchases were Bedford SB/Duple Vegas, although second-hand vehicles were often AECs or Daimlers. Latterly, Bedford VAM, VAL, YRQ and YRT models were favoured.

983 HHT was one of 10 SB1/Duples delivered in 1960 to be withdrawn in 1973/4. It is seen empty at Plymouth, possibly off Associated Motorways duplicate service, a duty often undertaken by Wessex vehicles. The driver in uniform with peaked cap is a vanished touch! *Peter Tulloch*

Right: Leather's Coaches, of Maiden Bradley, in Wiltshire, operated this Plaxton-bodied Bedford SB5, seen passing the gardens at Stourhead in 1988. The cross dates back to 1373, previously standing in two locations in Bristol, before being re-erected here in 1765. *Tony Moyes*

LEATHERS

The Bristol LH variants were in production between 1968 and 1983, and many were bodied as coaches, although most of these were sold to the private sector. British Airways bought its only LHs in 1980/1, these being five Plaxton-bodied LHS6Ls (RLN 227-31W). RLN 231W later passed to North Devon independent Taw & Torridge, and is seen unloading in Boutport Street, Barnstaple, having arrived on the 09.10 Fridays-only journey from Roborough in August 1998. RLN 231W still operated with Taw & Torridge in 2000, although this service is now run by Turner's Tours, Chulmleigh, and terminates at the new bus station at Belle Meadow. *Kevin Lane*

Greenslades Tours, based in Torquay, favoured the AEC Reliance for most new coaches between 1958 and 1970, although the first had been bought back in 1955. In 1961, however, only three were added to the fleet, together with four Fords. This trio carried Harrington Cavalier bodies and lasted a very respectable 12 years with Greenslades. 541 CFJ (fleetnumbers were not carried until 1971) sits in the morning sunshine at Land's End in July 1967. After withdrawal, 404, as it had become, spent most of the following 10 years as a non-PSV with a school, and then sadly went for scrap. *Mike A. Sutcliffe*

Above: The classic Royal Blue image at Exeter: LTA 897 is parked in the city, on layover from a London service in the summer of 1962. Part of the Southern National fleet and numbered 1268, LTA 897 is a 1950 Bristol LL6B with Duple bodywork. It lasted in service one more year, and was scrapped in 1964. *Mike A. Sutcliffe*

Right: Britain's coaching scene 30 years ago: a representative selection of vehicles at Plymouth in July 1969, including AEC Reliances, Bedford SBs and VAMs, a Bristol MW, Fords, and Leyland Tiger Cubs and Leopards. Bodywork appears to include Duple, ECW, Harrington, Plaxton and Willowbrook. One suspects that a similar view today would consist mainly of Volvo B10Ms, with even Leylands and Bedfords thin on the ground. *Colin Martin*

W.FARRELL LTD
GUERNSEY TOM
BRETONSIDE
GREY CARS
940 GTA
RHT 920G
220 HUM

Above: An interesting 1960s line-up at the premises of W. P. Cocks, St Austell. The only bus on view is ex-North Western Road Car ECW-bodied Bristol L5G CDB 181, acquired in 1960. The two Bedford OBs are JOD 640 and HYN 470. Pride of place, however, goes to Tilling-Stevens LRL 7, which carried a Dutfield body; withdrawn in 1964, it sadly eluded preservation. *Photobus / Arnold Richardson*

Right: In the 1950s the Channel Islands were a marvellous hunting-ground for those after old and interesting buses and coaches. This Bedford WTB carried a Duple body and was new to Wiltshire operator A. W. Hadrell & Sons, Calne, in 1937, registered AMW 544. It came to Jersey in 1953, finding employment with Jersey Tours, St Helier. Jersey Tours had commenced operation in 1950 and by the time that this picture was taken, in the summer of 1959, was on to its third owner, Hill's Tours of West Bromwich. The WTB was withdrawn after the 1960 season, returned to the UK, and apparently disappeared without trace. Jersey Tours was sold to Tantivy Motors at the end of 1971. *Mike A. Sutcliffe*

JERSEY TOURS
COACH STATION
BOOKING OFFICE
AND WAITING ROOM
JERSEY TOURS
J 14532
CRAZY
nite

TRIDENT
CONTINENTAL
ARRIVALS
TANTIVY
MOTORS
J 35767
15
TANTIVY MOTORS
110
J 60698

Left: Tantivy Motors was an altogether older company, with horsebus origins dating back to 1897. The motorbus was introduced into the fleet in 1915. Tantivy's buses and routes passed to the major operator on the island, Jersey Motor Transport, in 1949, the company thereafter concentrating on its coaching activities. Further mergers and takeovers in the 1990s resulted in its becoming Tantivy Blue Coach Tours from 1996.

Tantivy's J 35767 was a Duple Dominant-bodied Bedford SB5, new in 1975 and seen awaiting arrivals at St Helier in May 1984, with Ford Transit J 60698 alongside. The Bedford was withdrawn 10 years later, and subsequently went for scrap. *Tony Moyes*

Above: A murky day at Coventry Pool Meadow finds Red & White Services Bristol RELH6G RC1066 (GWO 10D) on its way to Treherbert. This was among the first batch of RELHs for the company, which eventually bought 61 of the type. Alongside is North Western Road Car 411 (SJA 411K), heading north to Manchester. The date is November 1972. *John Jones*

Neath & Cardiff Luxury Coaches Ltd began in the 1930s and sold out to the BET group in 1951, retaining its separate identity. Known affectionately as the 'Brown Bombers', N&C's coaches plied their trade between Cardiff and Swansea, either via Neath or Briton Ferry bridge. In June 1963, KCY 490, one of the 1954 Guy Arab UFs, enters Bridgend bus station, Cardiff-bound. The centre-entrance Park Royal body allows a superb view from the front passenger seat next to the driver — something missing with a front entrance layout. At this time, most of the fleet was AEC, although a dozen of these Arab UFs were still in service. In 1971 Neath & Cardiff, by then running only AEC Reliances, was absorbed into the South Wales Transport fleet. *Philip Wallis*

A. E. & F. R. Brewer, based at Caerau, near Maesteg, was operating a bus way back in 1920. A mixed fleet has been operated over the years; JTG 854 is a 1949 Duple A-bodied AEC Regal III, while the bus behind is 212 FNY, an AEC Reliance with bodywork by Weymann. Both are seen at the depot in August 1963. *Mike A. Sutcliffe*

Below: Western Welsh once operated throughout much of South and West Wales, with depots as far apart as Cardiff and Fishguard. Its territory contracted during the 1960s, with much of that in West Wales passing to other operators. In April 1978 Western Welsh was merged with Red & White and Jones' Omnibus to form National Welsh, itself now only a memory following its post-deregulation demise.

Back in 1963, the Western Welsh fleet was mainly AEC and Leyland, with coaching rolling stock including AEC Regals and Reliances, together with a few Leyland Royal Tigers. GUH 521 was one of the latter — a 1953 Leyland PSU1/16 with Willowbrook bodywork — pictured in Carmarthen in the July. *Philip Wallis*

Right: The well-known independent, Silcox of Pembroke Dock, began bus operation in 1933 by taking over J. R. Ford of Pembroke. Postwar, the purchase of new and (later) second-hand Bristols, together with rebuilding and rebodying activities, brought Silcox to the attention of enthusiasts. Many other interesting vehicles have been used over the years; OHA 298 was a 1950 AEC Regal III with a Harrington body, new in 1950 to Gliderways Coaches, Smethwick, although it didn't reach Pembroke Dock until 1958, lasting in the fleet for nearly 10 years. *Mike A. Sutcliffe*

PRIVATE
SILCOX
OHA 298

Above: Rees, of Crymmych, south of Cardigan, bought one new coach in 1972 — Duple-bodied Ford R192 CDE 600K. Ten years later it was still going strong; judging by the hills encountered, like this one at Glog, Rees certainly got his money's-worth out of the vehicle! *John Jones*

Right: Crosville bought a number of Bedford OBs in the early postwar period, including Duple-bodied MFM 39 in 1950. Withdrawn in 1959, it passed to Davies, Llanfihangel-yng-Gwynfa, in Montgomeryshire, along with three others. Only MFM 39 was actually used by Davies, the others being sold on. In May 1969 it is seen crossing the Vyrnwy Dam, working a Saturday journey from Llanwddyn to Oswestry. Davies sold the Bedford a couple of months later, but, unlike most other vehicles illustrated in these pages, it has survived, eventually passing into preservation in 1975. *Tony Moyes*

The Ulster Transport Authority was set up to bring together Northern Ireland's road and rail services, and lasted almost 20 years, from 1948 to 1967 when bus interests of the UTA passed to Ulsterbus. The first new coaches for UTA in any numbers were a batch of Leyland Tiger Cubs, bodied by UTA, delivered in 1957, while the AEC Reliance subsequently found favour. Only one coach was bought in 1964, 144 GZ, a 21-seat UTA-bodied Bedford VAS, seen in Belfast when new. In 1967 it received 20 bus seats and was converted to one-man operation. *Mike A. Sutcliffe*

In contrast to 1964, the Ulster Transport Authority took only coaches in 1965, these being 35 Bedford SB5s with Duple bodies and a quartet of Leyland PSU3 Leopards, all with bodywork by UTA. (Two further Leopards followed in 1966.) The Leopards were built for express services between Belfast and Omagh, Belfast and Enniskillen, and Londonderry and Dublin, all under the 'Wolfhound' name. 2481 OZ, the first of the batch, is pictured in Belfast. *Mike A. Sutcliffe*

In 1966 certain unremunerative UTA routes passed to other operators, including those in Portrush, which went to new operator Coastal Bus Services Ltd. Leyland Royal Tigers found favour in the early years, including this ex-Southdown Duple-bodied example, NCD 661. *Mike A. Sutcliffe*

TOURING
Dublin Hire Coaches
CZO 23
GZI
754
Dublin Hire Coaches

Left: Only three Bristol RELHs — two coaches and a bus — were supplied new to Irish operators. The first of this trio was CZO 23, a Plaxton-bodied RELH6L bought by Dublin Hire Coaches in 1968. Formed in 1963, the fleet had already acquired second-hand Bristols from the UK, the new vehicles being bought in response to an increase in continental touring. *Mike A. Sutcliffe*

Above: The last train on the narrow-gauge Londonderry & Lough Swilly Railway ran in 1953, although the company was running its first bus as early as 1929. Indeed, buses are still running today. Many former UK buses have ended their days in this corner of Ireland, but here I can illustrate just one. North Western Road Car sold several of its first underfloor-engined coaches — all-Leyland Royal Tiger PSU1/15s new in 1952 — to the L&LSR in 1963. Re-registered IU 9514 was originally FDB 609 when working for NWRCC, and is seen at what had been the most northerly railway station in Ireland, Cardonagh, in County Donegal, in August 1964. *Mike A. Sutcliffe*

There has been, and indeed still is, a steady flow of buses and coaches passing to Irish operators from the UK. In earlier times, many would retain their original registrations, as illustrated here by Strachans-bodied Leyland Comet HRK 904, owned by Suirway, Knockroe, Passage East, County Waterford. New to a Croydon operator in 1950, it arrived fourth-hand at Suirway in 1963 and was photographed at Waterford three years later. The coach on the right is another Suirway vehicle — Whitson-bodied AEC Regal III GBU 5, new to Shearings, also in 1950. *Mike A. Sutcliffe*